# VETERANS *DAY*

## Joanna Ponto

**Enslow Publishing**
101 W. 23rd Street
Suite 240
New York, NY 10011
USA

enslow.com

Published in 2017 by Enslow Publishing, LLC.
101 W. 23rd Street, Suite 240, New York, NY 10011

**Library of Congress Cataloging-in-Publication Data**

Names: Ponto, Joanna, author.
Title: Veterans Day / Joanna Ponto.
Description: New York, NY : Enslow Publishing, 2017. | Series: The story of our holidays | Includes bibliographical references and index. | Audience: Age 10 and up. | Audience: Grade 4 to 6.
Identifiers: LCCN 2016001039| ISBN 9780766076402 (library bound) | ISBN 9780766076389 (pbk.) | ISBN 9780766076396 (6-pack)
Subjects: LCSH: Veterans Day--Juvenile literature.
Classification: LCC D671 .P66 2016 | DDC 394.264--dc23
LC record available at http://lccn.loc.gov/2016001039

Printed in the United States of America

**To Our Readers:** We have done our best to make sure all website addresses in this book were active and appropriate when we went to press. However, the author and the publisher have no control over and assume no liability for the material available on those websites or on any websites they may link to. Any comments or suggestions can be sent by e-mail to customerservice@enslow.com.

Portions of this book originally appeared in the book *Veterans Day: Remembering Our War Heroes* by Elaine Landau.

**Photo Credits:** Cover, p. 1 Vstock LLC/Getty Images; p. 4 Education Images/Universal Images Group/Getty Images; p. 6 Michael Sugrue/Stone/Getty Images; p. 8 Archive Photos/Getty Images; p. 10 US Government/Eisenhower Presidential Library and Museum/Wikimedia Commons/72-901-1 HR7786 Veterans Day June 1 1954.jpg/public domain; p. 11 Cynthia Farmer/Shutterstock.com; p. 14 Boston Globe/Getty Images; p. 16 Allen Lee Lake/Shutterstock.com; p. 18 VickyHart/iStock/Thinkstock; p. 19 mandritoiu/Shutterstock.com; p. 21 Tacoma News Tribune/Tribune News Service/Getty Images; p. 24 Chris So/Toronto Star/Getty Images; p. 26 Joel Sartore/National Geographic/Getty Images; p. 27 HUANG Zheng/Shutterstock.com; p. 29 Cheryl Wells.

# Contents

Veterans Day is a time to honor the men and women who have fought for the freedoms we enjoy as Americans.

# Fighting for Freedom

The people of the United States of America live in a free nation. Among the freedoms enjoyed by Americans is religious freedom. Americans can pray at a church, a temple, or a mosque—or not pray at all. It is up to them.

People in the United States can also live where they want. They can pick any job they are able to do. They can even own a business.

Americans are free to travel, too. They can go anywhere. They do not need the government's permission. People in the United States love their freedoms. But they know that other people worked very hard for those freedoms.

Brave men and women have fought for America's freedom. These people have been members of the United States armed

The men and women in the armed forces risk their lives fighting to maintain our freedom. Many have have served in dangerous combat missions all over the world.

forces. The armed forces are made up of the men and women in the U.S. Army, Navy, Marines, Air Force, and Coast Guard.

Veterans are members of the United States armed forces who have served the country at home and abroad. Some have fought in a war.

America is very grateful for its soldiers. All are heroes. Some died fighting for their country. But they all fought to protect the rights and freedom of American citizens.

We show our respect for our veterans on a special day known as Veterans Day. Veterans Day is celebrated each year on November 11.

On Veterans Day, America thanks its veterans. There are parades. People place flowers on soldiers' graves. Veterans Day is a day to remember and thank the people who have kept our nation free.

# Chapter 2

# A Day to Thank Our Soldiers

Americans have fought for their country since they fought for independence from England in the Revolutionary War. But America has not always had Veterans Day as a way to say thank you. This holiday began after World War I.

## World War I

World War I was fought between the years 1914 and 1918. There were many reasons for this war. A number of nations had become enemies. Each wanted to be the most powerful. Some wanted more land. That meant taking land belonging to other countries. It also meant going to war to get the land.

Most of the fighting in World War I took place in Europe. About ten million soldiers from both sides were killed, and

This photo shows a group of Allied soldiers celebrating the news that World War I had ended. The war had taken a tremendous toll on both sides.

at least twenty million more were wounded.

Early on November 11, 1918, the countries fighting the war agreed to make peace. At 11 a.m. that day, the fighting stopped. Soldiers on battlefields put down their guns. They cheered and blew whistles. The good news spread around the world. People hugged one another and danced in the streets. Some businesses closed. The owners and workers wanted to celebrate the end of the war, too.

## Armistice Day

Americans were glad the war was over. But they did not forget those who had fought. These soldiers were remembered the next year. On

November 11, 1919, President Woodrow Wilson declared the day Armistice Day. It was the anniversary of the end of World War I and a day to honor the war's veterans.

Americans wanted Armistice Day to be an official holiday. People wrote to their lawmakers to ask them to help. In 1926, November 11 was officially named Armistice Day. Twelve years later, in 1938, our lawmakers made Armistice Day a federal holiday. This meant government offices were closed and there was no mail delivery. Schools, banks, and libraries were also closed.

## Veterans Day

World War I had been called the war to end all wars. People hoped there would never be another war. But soon different countries began fighting again. There were more wars.

That meant that there were other veterans, too. US soldiers fought bravely in World War II and the Korean War. Many Americans thought there should be a holiday to honor all veterans, not just those who had fought in World War I. Once again, they asked their leaders to help. In 1954, President Dwight D. Eisenhower signed an important bill. November 11 became known as Veterans Day.

On June 1, 1954, President Dwight Eisenhower signed HR7786, which officially changed Armistice Day to Veterans Day.

Later, Americans would fight in the Vietnam War, the Persian Gulf War, the Iraq War, and the War in Afghanistan. They often went to distant lands to keep the peace. Sometimes they died trying.

Veterans Day became a time to remember all those who served in the United States armed forces. People who died are remembered. So are the soldiers who came home.

## Tomb of the Unknowns

Each year, veterans are honored at the Tomb of the Unknowns. The Tomb of the Unknowns is near the center of Arlington National Cemetery. It faces the Potomac River and Washington, DC A soldier who died in World War I was placed in the tomb on November 11, 1921. No one knows his name. His body could not be identified. He stands for all of the World War I soldiers who died.

In 1958, two more soldiers were buried there. One had died in World War II. The other was killed in the Korean War. In 1984, a fourth soldier was also buried there. He died in the Vietnam War.

Each year on Veterans Day, a ceremony is held at the Tomb of the Unknowns. It always takes place on November 11 at exactly 11 a.m.

Etched on the tomb are the words "He rests in honored glory/An American soldier known but to God."

## Day Is Done

A bugle call known as "Taps" was written during the time of the American Civil War and is still played today.

### Taps

Fading light dims the sight,
And a star gems the sky, gleaming bright.
From afar drawing nigh-falls the night.

Day is done, gone the sun,
From the lake, from the hills, from the sky.
All is well, safely rest, God is nigh.

Then good night, peaceful night,
'Til the light of the dawn shineth bright,
God is near, do not fear—Friend, good night.

The time and date are important. World War I stopped at 11 a.m. on November 11, 1918. That was the eleventh hour of the eleventh day of the eleventh month.

All the different military groups take part in the ceremony. There are two minutes of silence. No one speaks during that time out of respect for the dead soldiers.

A wreath is placed at the tomb by the president of the United States. A military bugle song called "Taps" is played. Everyone stands quietly. It is a sad but important time. On Veterans Day, people remember those who died for America's freedom.

# Chapter 3

# Celebrating Veterans Day

The American people are thankful for those who have served their country. They owe these men and women a great debt. They want the veterans to know how they feel.

The ceremony at the Tomb of the Unknowns is important. But there are also many other ways to say thank you on Veterans Day.

## Ceremonies

Many events are planned by veterans' groups. The members of these groups are veterans. They have joined together to work on different projects. Men and women who are still

Past and present members of the US armed forces may travel from great distances to march in Veterans Day parades.

in the military usually help. They, too, are a part of Veterans Day ceremonies.

Some ceremonies take place at soldiers' gravesites. People across America gather at military cemeteries. Often they are the families of veterans. Friends and neighbors sometimes come, too. Veterans may also attend these ceremonies. They can talk about what happened to them in wartime. Elected officials are usually there. They give speeches, too. Flowers are placed on soldiers' graves.

## Veterans Day Parades

Veterans are remembered in other ways, as well. In many places there are Veterans Day parades. Veterans' groups march in the parades. So do other people. High school marching bands play music. The songs show our pride in America.

There may be military vehicles and floats in the parade, also. Floats may show patriotic scenes. They may be decorated with American flags and red, white, and blue streamers.

Thousands of people march in New York City's Veterans Day parade. Veterans Day parades are always popular. Everyone cheers for the marchers. People clap as the different veterans' groups pass. Some people wave small American flags. They are proud of our nation's military.

Some Veterans Day parades are large like the one in New York City is. Other parades are small. Some communities have a lot of military and veterans. Others have very few. Many veterans of the older wars,

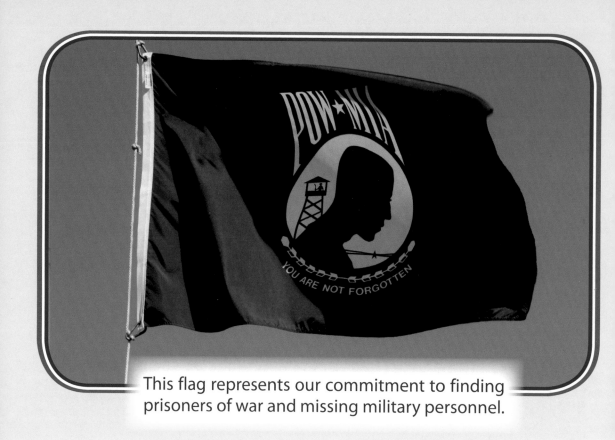

This flag represents our commitment to finding prisoners of war and missing military personnel.

such as World War II and Korea, have died. Others have become too old or too ill to march.

# POW-MIA

Many parades display POW-MIA flags. POW stands for Prisoner of War. These are soldiers who were taken prisoner by the enemy. MIA stands for Missing in Action. These are soldiers who were lost in battle. No one knows what happened to them. They might have been taken prisoner, or they might have been killed. Their bodies were never found.

POW-MIA flags are often seen at Veterans Day events. They remind us not to forget these brave soldiers. It is important to remember all our veterans.

Some people do this by wearing a special flower made of red paper on Veterans Day. The flowers are called poppies. They are sold by a group called the Veterans of Foreign Wars (VFW). VFW members help us remember other veterans. The money is used to help veterans.

The poppy has a special meaning. It was the subject of a famous poem called "In Flanders Fields," which was written by a soldier on the battlefield in World War I. The soldier was a doctor who treated many dying men. Yet all around him poppies grew. That is because the flower only grows in rooted-up soil. The soil on battlefields is like that. Now poppies are a reminder of the soldiers who died.

## Other Forms of Celebration

Libraries often put out books about war on Veterans Day. There may also be books about military life. Museums show weapons and

# Wartime Apple Brown Betty*

During World War II many foods, such as sugar and flour, were heavily rationed. This means people were only allowed to buy a small amount each week so the government could make sure there was enough food for everyone. People had to learn to make recipes with different ingredients. This recipe replaced the all-American apple pie.

## Ingredients:

2 cups (120 g) bread cubes
6 tablespoons (90 g) butter or margarine, melted
6 cups (900 g) sliced apples
1 cup (240 mL) honey or maple syrup
1 teaspoon (5 mL) cinnamon
zest of 1 lemon
¼ cup (60 mL) cold water

## Directions:

1. Preheat the oven to 350°F (175°C).
2. Mix the bread cubes and melted butter together with a wooden spoon or spatula.
3. In a separate bowl, mix together the honey or syrup, cinnamon, lemon zest, and water with a wooden spoon or spatula.
4. Grease a baking pan with oil or butter. Spread 1/3 of the bread cubes on the bottom of the pan. Lay half the apples on top of the bread cubes, then pour on half the honey mixture.
5. Spread the second third of the bread cubes on top of the apple layer. Top this layer of bread cubes with the rest of the apples and the honey mixture.
6. Spread the rest of the bread cubes on top of this.
7. Bake for 35-40 minutes until the top is brown and you can easily poke a toothpick or fork through the apples.

* Adult supervision required.

The Empire State Building in New York City honors veterans by changing their display lights to red, white, and blue.

military uniforms. Letters that soldiers sent home during wars are also shown.

Bakeries sell Veterans Day cakes and cupcakes. These have red, white, and blue frosting. Many places sell cookies in the shape of the American flag. People at home may bake American treats. Try making an apple brown Betty using the recipe on page 18.

On Veterans Day, businesses and homeowners alike may fly the American flag.

The Empire State Building in New York City honors the day, too. On Veterans Day, it is lit up in red, white, and blue. It can be seen for miles. Veterans Day is a day for people all across the country to remember and thank veterans.

# Chapter 4

# Celebrations in School

Veterans Day isn't only celebrated in the community. Many schools put on special programs to honor veterans, too. School bands may perform. They might play military marches. School choirs might sing patriotic songs, such as "America the Beautiful."

Sometimes veterans come to schools to speak to students. Young people learn what it is like to be a soldier, a fighter pilot, or a naval officer. Students also learn about being wounded. They find out how it feels to lose a friend in battle.

# Armed Forces Past and Present

One Veterans Day program was extra special. It took place in Stamford, Connecticut. Twenty-two veterans came to Stamford High School. All had once been students at the school nearly sixty years before. They had left before finishing school to fight in World War II. Now they were back to receive their high school diplomas. It was a wonderful ceremony. Hundreds of students were there. Families, friends, and city officials came, too.

The audience stood up when the veterans came in. Students walked the men to the stage. Everyone clapped. Everyone was glad

Many schools have Veterans Day assemblies to honor past and present military personnel. They may invite local veterans to discuss their experiences.

to be there. The high school principal said, "We must not miss this opportunity to say thank you." Everyone was proud of the veterans.

Schools may also receive visits from servicemen and servicewomen who are in the military today. At one school, US Marines came dressed in combat gear. Jeeps, cargo trucks, and tanks were also displayed. Students got a close-up view.

## Artistic Expressions

At times, schools have Veterans Day poster contests in which students make their own posters. Some draw soldiers or battle scenes. Their artwork shows what our veterans mean to us.

Art is often part of other Veterans Day school projects. Students in Fort Wayne, Indiana, remembered veterans through art. They made a wall of stars. First, they cut paper stars out of red, white, and blue paper. Then, they wrote the name of a different veteran on each star. The stars were put on the cafeteria wall. The students used the stars to make an American flag. Veterans who saw the wall were very proud.

In many schools, students write about Veterans Day. They write about why the holiday is important. The best writing may be read at school programs. In some schools, the students' work is posted on bulletin boards so everyone can read it.

Schools' newspapers write about Veterans Day, too. Student reporters may speak to veterans. The veterans might be family members or people in the community. The reporters write about the veterans' experiences. These make very interesting stories.

## A Patriotic Song

One of the most patriotic songs we sing today is called "America the Beautiful." It was written in 1913 by Katharine Lee Bates to show her feelings about our country.

### America the Beautiful

Oh beautiful, for spacious skies,
For amber waves of grain,
For purple mountain majesties
Above the fruited plain!
America! America!
God shed his grace on thee
And crown thy good with brotherhood
From sea to shining sea!

## How to Say Thank You

Veterans Day is a day to remember and thank our veterans. Often, students find ways to do this. They may make thank-you cards. On the

Veterans Day is celebrated in Canada, too. These kids wrote the names of Canadians who have been killed in action.

outside they might draw a soldier or a flag. Inside, they write a thank-you message. Their teacher takes the cards to a veterans' hospital.

Veterans like getting these special cards on their holiday. The cards show the veterans that people have not forgotten they fought for the freedom of America.

# Chapter 5

# Honoring Our Veterans

Over the last century and more, US veterans have been called on to serve their country. From World War I, when Veterans Day began, to the more recent War on Terror, the men and women of the armed forces have come to our nation's defense. How can we possibly show our gratitude and respect?

## World War II Vets

In 2000, the US Postal Service put out three new stamps for Veterans Day. All the new stamps honored World War II veterans.

Veterans Day 2000 was important for another reason. Work on the World War II Memorial in Washington, DC, began then. A memorial is a monument or statue that is a reminder of a person or event. This memorial honors World War II veterans. There are more than sixteen million veterans from World War II.

The National World War II Memorial in Washington, DC, opened in 2004.

Former president Bill Clinton dug the first few shovelfuls of earth to start the building. Military bands played. There were large television screens at the site. They showed scenes from World War II. Many people had looked forward to that day. For thirteen years, they had raised money for the memorial.

One of those people was a wounded Vietnam veteran named Tom Schepers. No one expected Schepers to walk again, but he even learned to run. In 2000, he went on a special run to honor World World II veterans. The run began on June 6. Schepers started out from Camp Pendleton, a marine training base in California. The run ended on Veterans Day at the World War II Memorial in Washington, DC. He had run more than 3,300 miles (5,310 km)!

This was a wonderful way to honor US veterans. But you don't have to do anything so dramatic. Any time you see a veteran or someone in a military uniform, simply walk up to him or her and thank him or her for their service.

Veterans Day is an important time for veterans. But it is also a special day for all Americans. It is a day to honor those who protect us.

Veterans Day is a time to thank those who have fought for our freedom.

# Veterans Day Craft*

Make a thank-you card to give to a veteran on Veterans Day. You might give it to a member of your family who is a veteran. You can also give it to someone else. Any veteran will be glad to know you care.

## Here are the supplies you will need:

a piece of blue construction paper
red and silver star stickers
a black marker
a stack of old magazines
safety scissors
white glue

## Directions:

1. Fold the piece of blue paper in half from one short end to the other. This is your card.

2. Decorate the outside of the card with the star stickers.

3. Use the black marker to write the words "THANK YOU" on the front of the card.

4. Think about why you are grateful to our veterans. Then look through the magazines. Find the picture that best shows your feelings.

5. Cut the picture out and glue it inside your card.

6. Write your own message next to the picture.

# Veterans Day Thank-You Card

*Safety Note: Be sure to ask for
help from an adult, if needed,
to complete this project.

# Glossary

armistice—An agreement to stop fighting.

bill—A plan for a new law.

century—One hundred years.

democracy—A government that is run by the people who live under its rules.

emblem—A symbol that stands for an idea.

memorial—A reminder of a person or an event.

mosque—A sacred place to pray for Muslims.

patriotic—Showing love for one's country.

truce—An agreement by enemies to stop fighting.

veteran—A person who has served in the armed forces.

# Learn More

## Books

Dash, Meredith. *Veterans Day*. Minneapolis, MN: ABDO Kids, 2015.

Dayton, Connor. *Veterans Day*. New York, NY: PowerKids Press, 2012.

Murray, Julie. *Veterans Day*. Edina, MN: ABDO Publishing Company, 2012.

Pettiford, Rebecca. *Veterans Day*. Minneapolis, MN: Jump!, Inc., 2016.

## Websites

**Department of Veterans Affairs: Veterans Day Homepage**

va.gov/opa/vetsday

*This official website for the Veterans Association provides information about Veterans Day celebrations and promotions each year.*

**Enchanted Learning's Veterans Day Activities**

enchantedlearning.com/crafts/veterans

*This site has lots of Veterans Day craft ideas, printable books, worksheets, puzzles, and more.*

**Infoplease Page on Veterans Day**

infoplease.com/spot/veteransday1.html

*Go to this page for information on veterans' statistics, the medal of honor, history of the holiday, and more.*

# Index